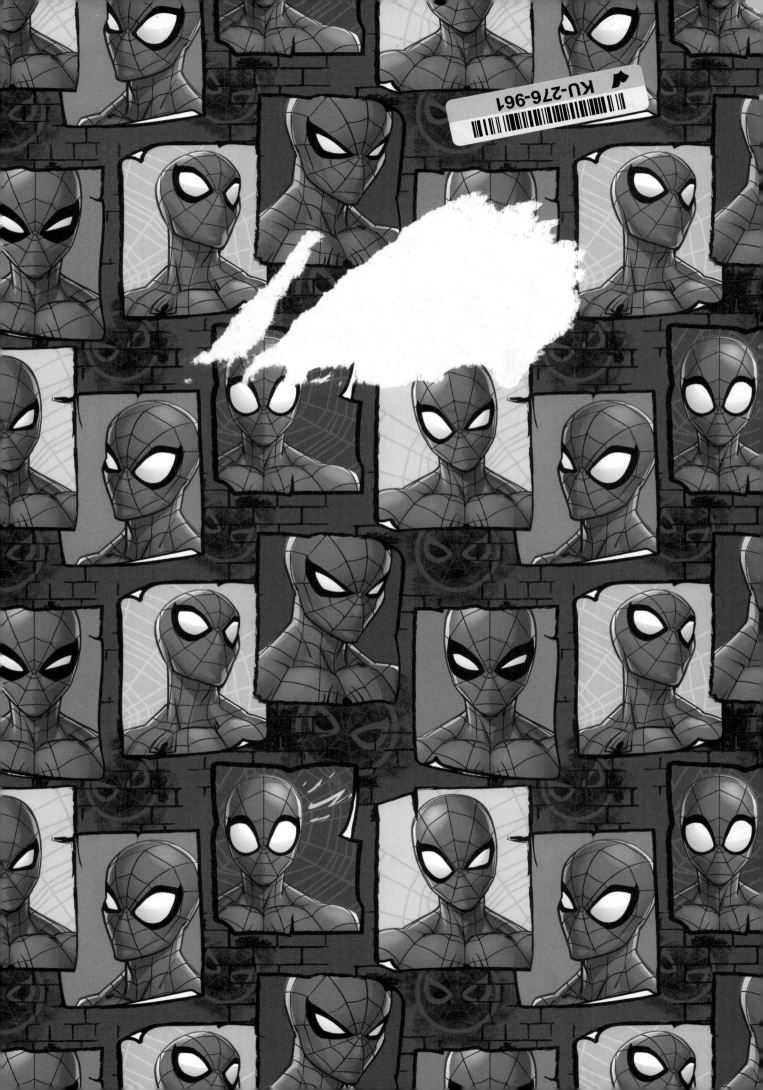

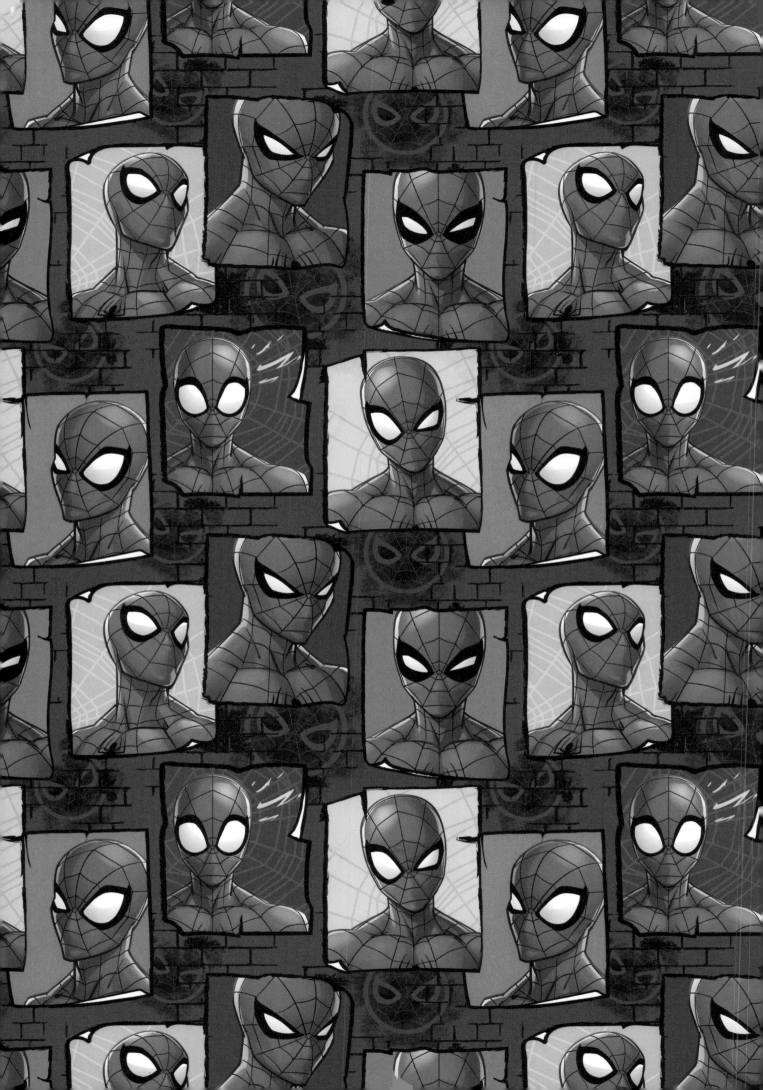

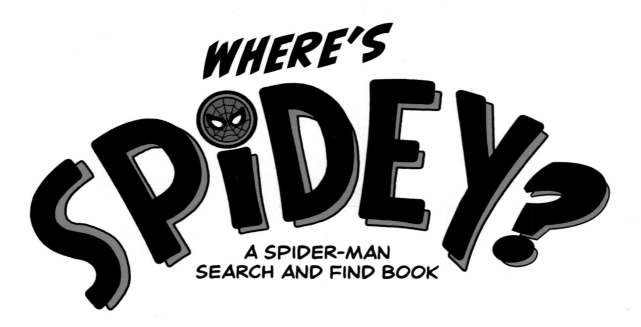

A SPIDER-MAN
SEARCH AND FIND BOOK

STUDIO
PRESS

First published in the UK in 2019 by Studio Press Books,
an imprint of Bonnier Books UK,
The Plaza, 535 King's Road, London, SW10 0SZ

studiopressbooks.co.uk
bonnierbooks.co.uk

© 2019 MARVEL

Printed in Italy
1 3 5 7 9 10 8 6 4 2

ISBN 978-1-78741-557-7

Written by Emma Drage
Designed by Nia Williams
Illustrated by Marco D'Alfonso

*In memory of Chris Spencer*

# MEET SPIDEY!

INTRODUCING... SPIDER-MAN! MEET THE WALL-CLIMBING SUPER-HERO. YOU'LL FIND HIM AND THE REST OF THESE INCREDIBLE CHARACTERS (AND THE NOT-SO-INCREDIBLE J. JONAH JAMESON) HIDDEN IN EVERY SCENE. LOOK OUT FOR THEM AS YOU EXPLORE SPIDEY'S NEW YORK.

## SPIDER-MAN (PETER PARKER)

PETER PARKER GAINED HIS SPIDER-LIKE POWERS AFTER BEING BITTEN BY A RADIOACTIVE SPIDER. NOW, HE SPLITS HIS TIME BETWEEN ORDINARY HIGH SCHOOL LIFE AND SWINGING THROUGH THE STREETS OF NEW YORK, FIGHTING CRIME!

# SPIDER-MAN (MILES MORALES)

MILES MORALES SERVED AS SPIDER-MAN IN THE ULTIMATE UNIVERSE BEFORE HIS WORLD WAS ERASED FROM EXISTENCE AND HE WAS ADOPTED BY PETER PARKER'S EARTH.

# SPIDER-WOMAN

JESSICA DREW WAS TRAINED AS AN AGENT FOR THE SINISTER ORGANISATION HYDRA. SHE LATER CHANGED HER WAYS, BECOMING THE WORLD'S FIRST SPIDER-WOMAN.

# MARY JANE WATSON

A TALENTED ACTRESS, ADEPT AT COVERING UP HER BELOVED PETER PARKER'S DOUBLE LIFE. MJ IS KNOWN FOR HER COURAGE AND RESOURCEFULNESS IN THE FACE OF DANGER.

# J. JONAH JAMESON

THE OPINIONATED PUBLISHER OF THE DAILY BUGLE LOVES THE SOUND OF HIS OWN VOICE. HE'S EVEN GROUCHIER THAN HE LOOKS AND IS AN ANTI-SPIDER-MAN ACTIVIST.

# AUNT MAY

AFTER PETER PARKER'S PARENTS DIED, AUNT MAY AND HER HUSBAND DIDN'T HESITATE TO ADOPT HIM. AUNT MAY WAS OFTEN OVER-PROTECTIVE OF PETER AS A CHILD.

# SPIDEY IS MISSING!

NEW YORK CITY IS UNDER ATTACK! A HORDE OF DANGEROUS VILLAINS IS CAUSING MAYHEM AND THERE'S ONLY ONE PERSON WHO CAN STOP THEM – SPIDER-MAN! BUT WHERE IS HE? CAN YOU FIND SPIDEY BEFORE THE WHOLE CITY FALLS INTO CHAOS?

## GREEN GOBLIN

## MISTER NEGATIVE

## VULTURE

## CENTRAL PARK

## CHINATOWN

## SANDMAN

## AVENGERS TOWER

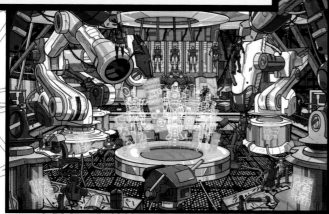

## KRAVEN THE HUNTER

## SPIDER-MAN NOIR

## DOCTOR OCTOPUS' LAB

## SPIDER-HAM

## WRESTLING RING

## MYSTERIO

## LIZARD

# GREEN GOBLIN

WITH HIS DEADLY PUMPKIN BOMBS, GREEN GOBLIN IS ONE OF THE MOST DANGEROUS VILLAINS ON THE PLANET. HELP IS NEEDED ON BROOKLYN BRIDGE TO STOP HIM IN HIS TRACKS... BUT WHERE'S SPIDEY?

# MISTER NEGATIVE

SOMETHING SUSPICIOUS IS HAPPENING AT THE DAILY BUGLE! MISTER NEGATIVE, THE BOSS OF A CRIMINAL UNDERGROUND NETWORK, HAS SNUCK INTO THE NEWSPAPER OFFICE. CAN YOU SPOT HIM?

# VULTURE

THERE'S TROUBLE UP ABOVE! VULTURE, THE ELDERLY ENGINEER WHO TURNED TO A LIFE OF CRIME WHEN HE CREATED A MIGHTY FLYING SUIT, IS TERRORIZING CITIZENS ON THE ROOFTOPS OF NYC.

# CENTRAL PARK

SPIDEY IS ENJOYING A MOMENT OF CALM IN CENTRAL PARK. CAN YOU SPOT HIM AS HE TAKES A BREAK FROM FIGHTING CRIME? LOOK OUT FOR OTHER FAMILAR FACES ENJOYING SOME DOWN-TIME.

# CHINATOWN

VENOM, THE ALIEN SYMBIOTE WITH A LIQUID-LIKE FORM, IS CREEPING THROUGH THE DARKNESS TO ATTACK CHINATOWN. CAN YOU FIND SPIDEY AND STOP VENOM FROM CAUSING CHAOS BEFORE IT'S TOO LATE?

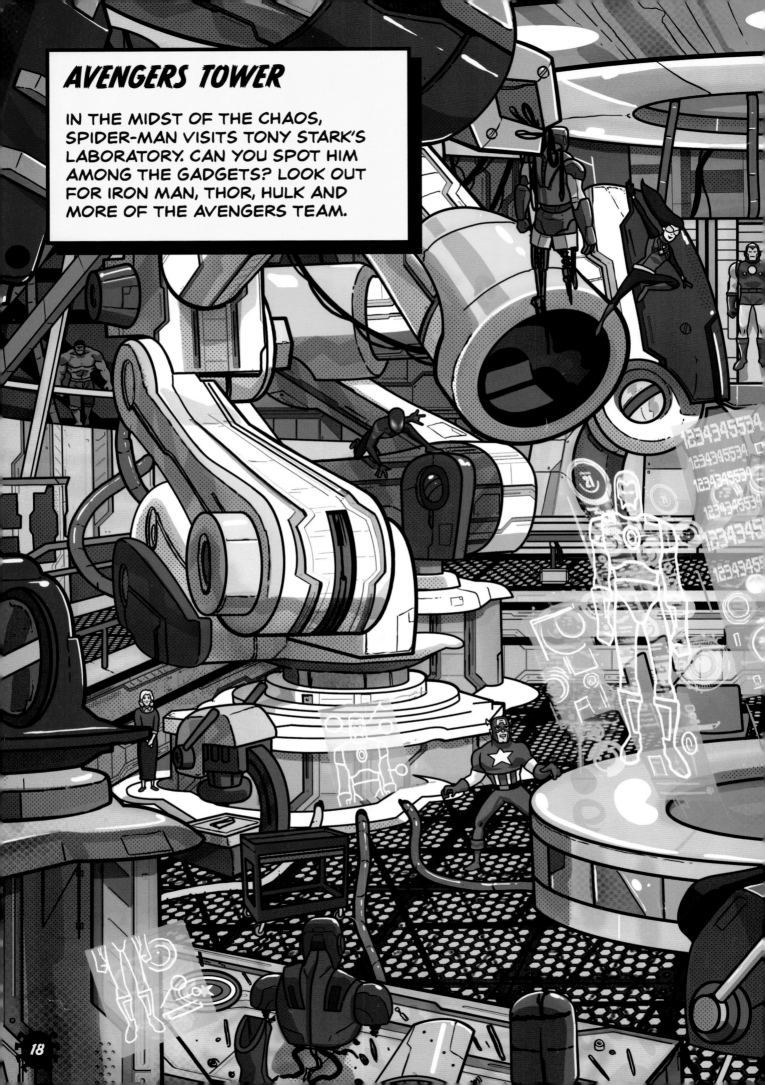

# AVENGERS TOWER

IN THE MIDST OF THE CHAOS, SPIDER-MAN VISITS TONY STARK'S LABORATORY. CAN YOU SPOT HIM AMONG THE GADGETS? LOOK OUT FOR IRON MAN, THOR, HULK AND MORE OF THE AVENGERS TEAM.

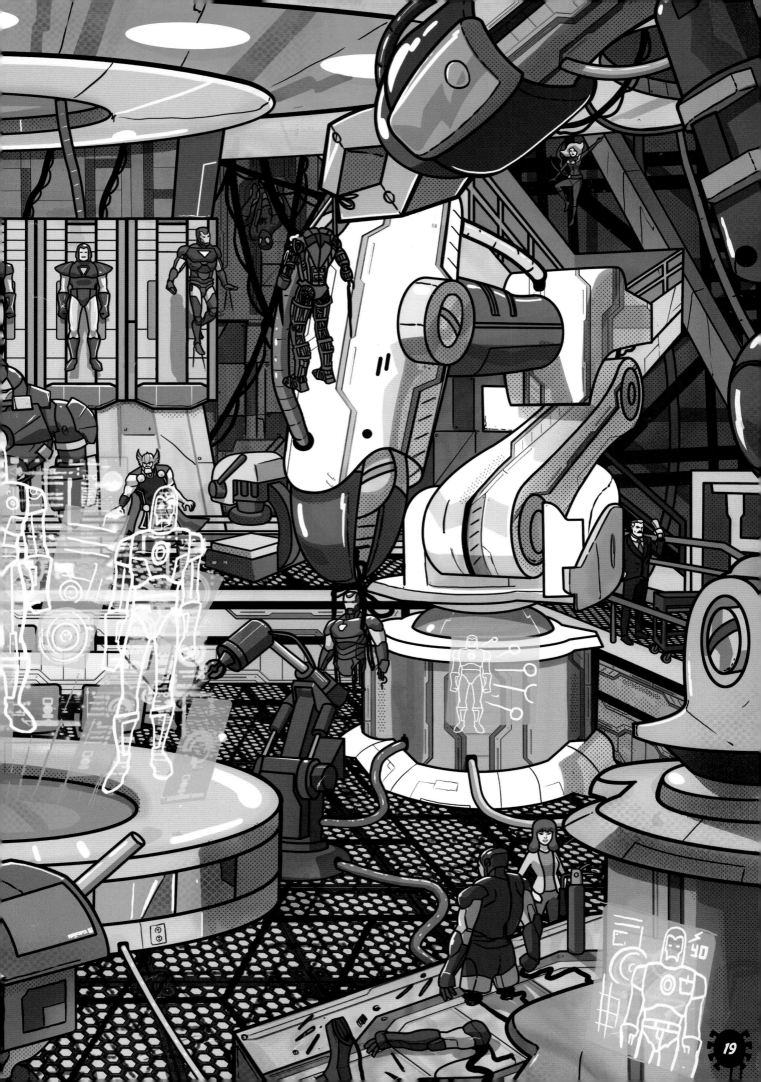

# KRAVEN THE HUNTER

THINGS ARE GETTING WILD AT CENTRAL PARK ZOO! KRAVEN THE HUNTER, A BRILLIANT ATHLETE WHO STALKS HIS PREY LIKE A JUNGLE CAT, IS CAUSING CHAOS. CAN SPIDER-MAN RESTORE ORDER?

# SPIDER-MAN NOIR

THINGS ARE GETTING DARK...
WELCOME TO NYC IN THE 1930S ON
EARTH-90214. LOOK OUT FOR WEB
WARRIOR MEMBER SPIDER-MAN
NOIR IN HIS TRADEMARK GOGGLES
AND EXPLOSION-PROOF SUIT.

# DOCTOR OCTOPUS' LAB

WITH A SCIENTIFIC MIND THAT RIVALS PETER PARKER'S, DOCTOR OCTOPUS IS SPIDER-MAN'S GREATEST FOE. WHAT SINISTER SCHEME IS COOKING UP IN HIS LABORATORY NOW, AND CAN SPIDEY STOP HIM?

# SPIDER-HAM

THE CITIZENS OF NYC ARE UNAWARE THAT SWINGING FROM SKYSCRAPER TO SKYSCRAPER ABOVE THEIR HEADS IS... SPIDER-HAM, THE TALKING HERO PIG, OTHERWISE KNOWN AS PETER PORKER.

# WRESTLING RING

SPIDER-MAN RETURNS TO THE PLACE WHERE IT ALL BEGAN TO TAKE ON RHINO, THE FORMIDABLE FOE WITH SUPER STRENGTH, NEARLY UNBREAKABLE SKIN AND HORNS THAT RIP THROUGH STEEL!

# MYSTERIO

THINGS ARE GETTING A LITTLE WEIRD! NOTHING IS QUITE WHAT IT SEEMS WHEN MYSTERIO, THE MOST ENIGMATIC OF SPIDER-MAN'S ENEMIES, IS AROUND. CAN YOU SPOT ANYTHING ODD IN THE SCENE?

# LIZARD

WITH HIS SHARP TEETH AND ABILITY TO REGENERATE, LIZARD IS A FEROCIOUS FOE. CAN YOU FIND SPIDER-MAN BEFORE THE BLOOD-THIRSTY LIZARD DESTROYS THE SEASONAL FESTIVITIES?

# MORE CHARACTERS AND OBJECTS TO SEARCH AND FIND

## GREEN GOBLIN

- GOBLIN'S PUMPKIN BOMBS
- CONSTRUCTION WORKER'S HELMET
- BALLOON
- GREEN BACKPACK
- COPY OF THE DAILY BUGLE
- TOURIST TAKING A PHOTOGRAPH
- SPIDER WEB
- 'OSCORP' DELIVERY TRUCK

## MISTER NEGATIVE

- CLOCK
- FAX MACHINE
- TRASH CAN
- WORLD MAP
- MISTER NEGATIVE
- CAMERA
- COFFEE MUG
- GREEN GOBLIN ON TV SCREEN

## VULTURE

- DECKCHAIR
- ROMANTIC DINNER FOR TWO
- STRING OF FAIRY LIGHTS
- BBQ GRILL
- SATELLITE DISH
- DOG EATING SAUSAGES
- DJ WITH HIS DECKS
- POTTED PLANT

## CENTRAL PARK

- JOGGER
- BABY IN A PRAM
- SOMEBODY DOING TAI CHI
- SOMEBODY MEDITATING
- DOG WALKER
- CYCLIST
- SQUIRREL
- BLUE JAY

## CHINATOWN

- A BLUE CHINESE LANTERN
- LUCKY CAT
- WINDOW OF PEKING DUCKS
- CHEF TAKING A BREAK
- DRAGON
- SOMEBODY EATING NOODLES
- SOMEBODY EATING FISH BALLS
- CARNAGE (A SYMBIOTE)

## SANDMAN

- BUSKER
- STREET ENTERTAINER ON STILTS
- HOT DOG VENDOR
- COMIC BOOK SHOP
- 'OSCORP' BILLBOARD
- NEWSPAPER VENDOR
- SHOCKER
- SOMEONE PEEPING OUT FROM UNDERNEATH A DRAIN COVER

## AVENGERS TOWER

- IRON MAN
- CAPTAIN AMERICA
- CAPTAIN MARVEL
- THOR
- HULK
- CAPTAIN AMERICA'S SHIELD
- THOR'S HAMMER
- IRON MAN'S ROBOT ARM

## KRAVEN THE HUNTER

- KRAVEN'S WHIP
- KRAVEN'S POISON-TIPPED DARTS
- SEA LION
- GORILLA
- MONKEYS
- LEOPARD
- PENGUINS
- SLOTH

## SPIDER-MAN NOIR

- POLICEMAN
- SPIDER-MAN NOIR
- RATS
- CAT
- MAN IN A TRILBY
- OLD-FASHIONED TAXI
- AIRSHIP
- GRAMOPHONE IN A WINDOW

## DOCTOR OCTOPUS' LAB

- MICROSCOPE
- TEST TUBES
- BUNSEN BURNER
- HALF-EATEN DOUGHNUT
- PIZZA BOX
- MOUSE
- HAZMAT MASK
- SAFETY GLOVES

## SPIDER-HAM

- SPIDER-HAM
- SPIDER-GWEN
- PRETZEL VENDOR
- WINDOW CLEANER
- PLANT POT ON FIRE ESCAPE
- FLORIST
- COUPLE HOLDING HANDS
- SPARE TYRE

## WRESTLING RING

- WHISTLE
- MICROPHONE
- TOWEL
- SODA DRINK
- ICE-CREAM VENDOR
- SPOTLIGHT WITH A SPIDER'S WEB
- BURGER
- ANTI-VENOM (A SYMBIOTE)

## MYSTERIO

- FOUR-EYED DOG
- GREEN CAT
- DOOR HALF WAY UP A BUILDING
- GUITAR CASE
- PURPLE TREE
- LEVITATING PEDESTRIAN
- STRANGE CLOCK
- STRANGE-COLOURED TRAFFIC LIGHTS

## LIZARD

- FOUR FESTIVE WREATHS
- PEDESTRIAN PULLING A SUITCASE
- RED SCARF
- CHILD THROWING A SNOW BALL
- MAN DRINKING HOT CHOCOLATE
- PEDESTRIAN CARRYING GIFTS
- PAIR OF ICE SKATES
- 'OSCORP' CARRIER BAG

# ANSWERS

SPIDER-MAN, MILES MORALES, SPIDER-WOMAN, MARY JANE, J.J.J. AND AUNT MAY ARE CIRCLED IN YELLOW, AND THE OTHER CHARACTERS AND OBJECTS TO SEARCH AND FIND ARE CIRCLED IN BLUE.

## GREEN GOBLIN

## MISTER NEGATIVE

## VULTURE

# CENTRAL PARK

# CHINATOWN

# SANDMAN

## AVENGERS TOWER

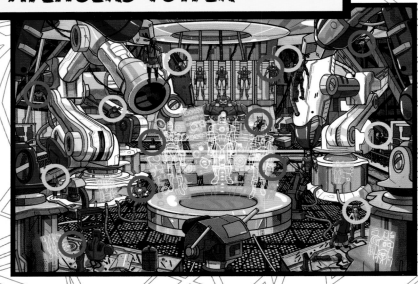

## KRAVEN THE HUNTER

## SPIDER-MAN NOIR

## DOCTOR OCTOPUS' LAB

## SPIDER-HAM

## WRESTLING RING

# MYSTERIO

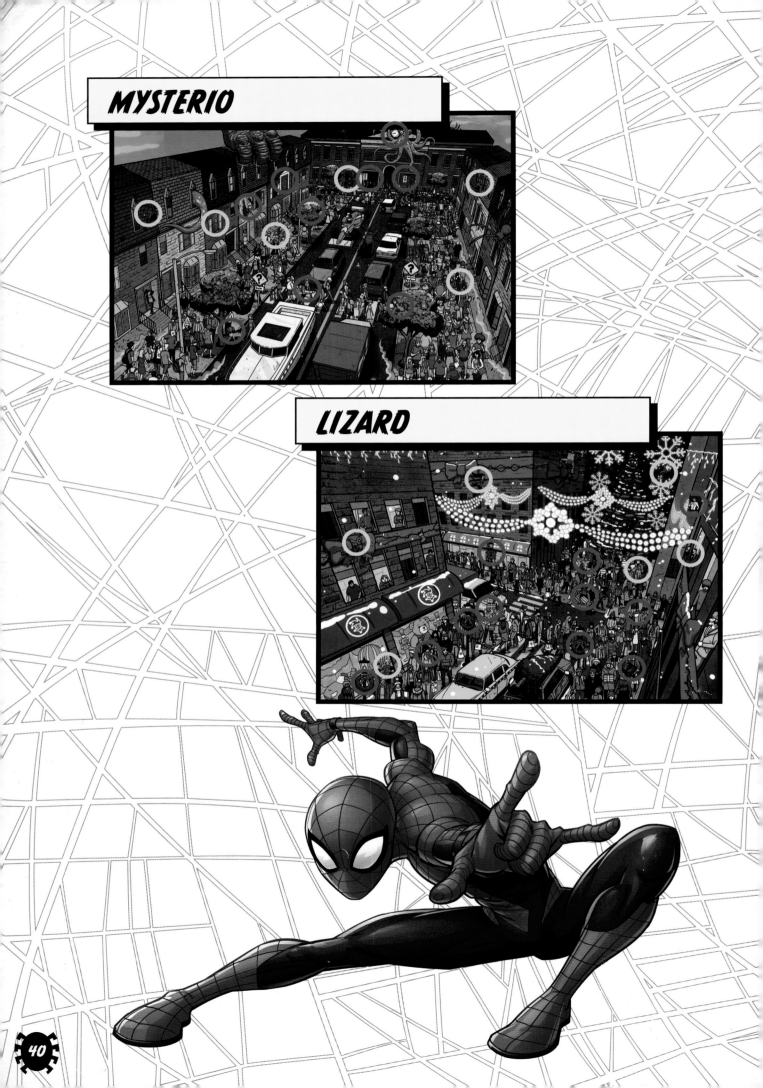

# LIZARD